RESILIENCE

Overcoming Obstacles with Mindfulness

Dr. Cenell Boch

RESILIENCE

Overcoming Obstacles with Mindfulness

Resilience: Overcoming Obstacles with Mindfulness

All rights are reserved. No part of this book may be used or reproduced in any manner without the copyright owner's written permission except for quotations in book reviews.

Copyright © 2024 Dr. Cenell Boch

ISBN: 978-1-959811-75-6 (Paperback)
ISBN: 978-1-959811-76-3 (Ebook)
Library of Congress Control Number: 2024919554

Book Cover Design: Okamoto
Interior Design: Amit Dey
Editor: Winsome Hudson
Author Photo Credit: Philip Dembinski

Website: www.wordeee.com
Twitter.com/wordeeeupdates
Facebook: facebook.com/Wordeee/
e-mail: contact@wordeee.com
Published by Wordeee in the United States, New York, New York 2024

Printed in the USA

ADVANCE PRAISE

Living a mindful life requires asking ourselves the right questions and reflecting on these questions with an open mind. In this book, Cenell Boch provides us with some of these important questions as a process of self-inquiry that can be used to help us become more aware of how our patterned thoughts and beliefs may be holding us back. By sharing her story and insights, the author gives us a relatable and real-life example of how mindfulness can transform suffering into an opportunity to grow and thrive. As a firm believer in the power of the mind, using Cenell's affirmations as a daily practice can allow the reader to begin to release long-held limiting beliefs and constricted conditioning, and instead create a path to living their full potential.

—Sheila Patel, MD,
Board Certified Family Physician
Chief Medical Officer for Chopra Global

I LOVE YOUR BOOK. You did a wonderful, amazing, and beautiful job of sharing your story in ways that empower and enlighten the reader and all of us. You are real and clear in your awesome way of communicating. You have an amazing story and journey to share. I am deeply inspired by you and what you have written.

—*Lynne Twist*
Author, The Soul of Money
Founder, The Soul of Money Institute

Resilience: Overcoming Obstacles with Mindfulness is a beacon of hope, blending the author's journey with practical wisdom. Through Dr. Boch's candid storytelling, readers will find inspiration and realize they're not alone in life's challenges. The book offers actionable advice, affirmations, and a journal for reflection. It's an essential Mindfulness roadmap for anyone seeking to overcome obstacles and embrace life with grace and resilience.

—*Janet Alston Jackson, Author*
A Cry for Light: A Journey Into Love
USA Book News Award winner

Wonderful things can come in small packages and *Resilience: Overcoming Obstacles with Mindfulness* is one of those "wonderful things." This small and mighty book provides a wealth of encouragement and practical tips for anyone experiencing depression, divorce, or loss. Dr. Cenell Boch shares what it means to transform trials into treasures in the midst of pursuing your dreams. This darling little book will delight and remind you there is life beyond the obstacles.

This book is for people ready to work on their Wellness Goals to increase self-awareness and self-confidence while decreasing stress and minimizing burnout.

—Pia Fitzgerald
The Wellness Tactician
Chief Executive Officer, WOW! Factor

I loved getting to know you better through your stories and journal entries. With heartfelt congratulations on realizing your dream of writing this book.

— Sara Ellis Conant
Co-Founder & CEO, a)plan Coaching

Dr. Cenell Boch's writing encourages us to remember that the Universe does not give us what we cannot handle. Her courage and candor shines through this book as she empowers readers with her lived experiences, questions for inquiry and affirmations for reflection. A must-read for anyone committed to growing in self-love and the service of a happier, healthier humanity.

— *Lynn Wong, NBC-HWC*
Founder LW Coaches

Dr. Boch's authenticity shines through, especially in her vulnerable journal entries, making this book feel like a conversation with a trusted friend. A must-read, a gift, a lifeline for anyone seeking to cultivate resilience, peace, and purpose in the face of life's obstacles."

—*Jesse Torrence*
Jesse Torrence Coaching
BA, Economics & International Relations, Stanford
MPA, International Development, Harvard

DEDICATION

To my irreplaceable family.
My beloved parents, Dan and
Bertha Munford, and my eleven siblings,
Vontella, John Robert, Victoria, Annie,
Margaret, Carolyn,
Ingram, Susan, Daniel Martin,
Chester (Khalil), and Bertha Marie.

Deepest gratitude and sincere love
to my husband, Wayne;
and to our children Richy, Daniel
Lindsey, Willie, and Samantha.

Thank you for helping me on my mindfulness journey.

TABLE OF CONTENTS

Dedication ix
Foreword xiii
Introduction xvii
Chapter 1 - Background 1
Chapter 2 - Knowledge: Preparing for My Life's Work .. 14
Chapter 3 - Finding Me 29
Chapter 4 - The BIG GLASS: Finding Peace of
    Mind With and Without Wine 38
Chapter 5 - Financial Peace 53
Chapter 6 - Surviving to Thriving to Simply Blessed 62
Chapter 7 - All You Ever Wanted Isn't Enough 76
Chapter 8 - Mindfulness 83
Chapter 9 - Mindfulness of Diversity and Inclusion..... 94
Affirmations for Your Daily Mindfulness Practice 106
Cenell's Dream 112
Resources 114
Acknowledgments 116
About the Author 118

FOREWORD

From the day that our mom brought Cenell home from the hospital after giving birth, I knew there was something special about her. The doctors told our parents that because she was born three months premature and weighed only 3.4 pounds, she would have delayed physical and mental development and she would walk, talk, and respond later than her peers. In fact, it was just the opposite! Cenell learned to walk, talk, and respond to our parents with no problems whatsoever. She was and is still considered a blessing to our family. She achieved excellent grades in elementary, middle, high school, and college. As a matter of fact, I'm sure if she were in school today, she would still receive good grades and excel.

Not only did she do well in school, but she also worked diligently with our church. She accepted Christ into her life at the age of -fifteen and considers herself a Christian. Cenell has worked with family, friends, and coworkers to improve their health, safety, and welfare. When Cenell was going through depression she would say little about what she was feeling. She never let on that she needed help, and focused on helping others in her family and community.

That is why this book is so important. When people find themselves at their lowest point dealing with obstacles, this book may help them understand and cope with life's challenges. Cenell provides an opportunity for us to learn about the challenges that we might face and to use those challenges as valuable life lessons. As you read this book, you will be able to see yourself in a new light. You will see yourself grow mentally and spiritually as you reflect on these life experiences. Cenell discusses the fact that no two people will experience life in the exact same way. However, in common humanity, we all want to live our best life despite challenges. This book will allow you to go within and reflect on a deep soul level about how you might navigate obstacles. The insights, guidance, and affirmations discussed in this book will provide hope and healing along with some humor.

As you read about the life-changing occurrences Cenell went through, I hope you become inspired to know that you have the power within you to overcome any obstacles that may come your way. I feel this book can and will help any person who is struggling…no matter how insurmountable the challenge seems. Know that you are supported on your journey and that there is another side. My hope is that as you read this book you feel loved, and respected, and have a deep understanding that we all matter.

Susan Munford-Amison, LSW, Retired
Beloved Sister of Cenell

INTRODUCTION

Greetings Dear Readers,

This book is not a memoir or a detailing of the trials and tribulations of my life, but rather a recollection of how I dealt with and faced head-on some of the most challenging times of my life. It is meant to be a pocketbook you can carry around for inspiration when needed. It includes my personal journal entries I wanted to share with you about my experiences with obstacles (depression and divorce) and how I have healed and recovered (or am still recovering) from these obstacles. Looking back over these periods of despair in my life, I began to realize how blessed I am. They say hindsight is 20/20 and, of course, it is. There are so many stories in my life I would love to share with you of how a way was made when seemingly no way was possible. Or stories of how just when I was about to give up instead all I did was say a small three-word prayer, *God Help Me*, and miraculously whether profound or in a very subtle way

I felt relief, a breath of fresh air, and a sense that everything was going to be all right.

We are similar in our humanness—so we all experience suffering, loss, pain, or hurt; joy, and happiness and strive to find fulfillment. At the end of the day, we all want to be LOVED, RESPECTED, ENGAGED IN OUR LIVES, and feel that we MATTER. And if you've lived long enough, I'm sure you too will underscore that none of us gets a pass on life's challenges. In my opinion, these challenges, no matter how difficult are meant to help us find our authentic selves. If you're up to the task, prodigious rewards await you.

In our human experiences, we all have things that make us similar, e.g., the commonality of the human body, the autonomic central nervous system's fight or flight response and so much more. We also have unique qualities such as our geographic location, customs, and circumstances of childhood or adulthood that make us different and experience life differently. All the circumstances we experience from our unique perspectives make us who we are. And though we may look alike on a macro level, on a micro level our genetic codes and our fingerprints differentiate us into unique human beings. For example, did you know that no two people of the almost nine billion who inhabit the world have the same fingerprint? What should that tell you about authenticity and uniqueness? So, though we experience similar things it is unlikely we experience the same situations, and finding solutions to our problems is a personal thing; yet we can learn how others have managed and adapt their solutions to fit our unique needs. Like you, I am not immune to life challenges and thankfully my life experiences and upbringing made me adaptable enough to find solutions that worked for me when I found myself depressed and anxious.

One of the great ways I found to access my authentic self is through journaling. And that's what I turned to when I found myself in a dark and unsafe space. This book invites you to go within and reflect at a soul level on how you might navigate the obstacles you will surely face in life. It will invite you to review times when you felt stuck and offer solutions on how to emerge triumphantly on the other side of tough circumstances. The insights, guidance, and remedies discussed in this book may provide hope and healing along with a bit of humor. I hope that you will read and re-read these pages to encourage your heart and mind to seek the beauty life has to offer. Please consider the tips outlined in this book as pearls of wisdom to reflect on. These pearls of wisdom may help you live a more fulfilling and peaceful life. May each life circumstance, self-reflection question, and affirmation bring you hope for a brighter tomorrow. Ultimately, I hope you use this book to strengthen your intention to live your best life to its highest possible expression.

This book will allow you to learn about the challenges I have faced and the lessons and techniques I have used to grow personally and spiritually. I hope you find -the lessons useful and I pray you choose PEACE, LOVE, and HAPPINESS.

I have included journal entries that I have made over my lifetime. They are not in chronological order but entered as they relate to overcoming obstacles. The journal entries are deeply personal and highlight my thought processes around the subjects in each chapter. They have been priceless in helping me organize my thoughts and feelings to write this book. I share particular stumbling blocks in my life, how I chose to deal with them, and how I came to be who I am today. They reflect how things occurred for me and how my spiritual maturation process developed.

At the end of each chapter, there is an opportunity to mindfully reflect on soul questions. Take your time completing these reflection questions. Write freely and often as you gain more awareness of yourself and your needs. These answers are for you and you alone. The reflection questions will allow you to take a deeper dive into applying mindful tips to your everyday life. There are no right or wrong answers, the questions are simply an opportunity for you to reflect on the material within each chapter to ascertain how the information could be applied to your unique life.

Many times, we intuitively know the answers to many tough life questions; however, because of subliminal conditioning, we might second-guess ourselves. I hope that this book provides the mind space and freedom for you to listen to your own North Star and gives you the courage to listen to your internal guidance system. We all have our beautiful intuition or guiding system within—I call it Source, God, Loving Awareness, Spirit, Nature, Universe. No matter what we call this internal guidance system, knowing it exists and that we can have the faith to call upon it, is what makes the difference and helps us in overcoming obstacles.

Lastly, there are mindfulness affirmations at the end of the book, where you are encouraged to read one affirmation for forty days and reflect on how these affirmations resonate with your daily life.

Thank you for taking the time to read and reflect on the affirmations and powerful journal entries that proved lifesaving for me. By adapting and using all or some of these mindful tools, I hope you will find joy and purpose in your life and move toward even greater happiness and health. Remember, the way we look at life is all about perspective and, I hope that like me, you will find that happiness is something you must find within yourself.

As you read about my life-changing occurrences, reflect on your life and know that you have the power inside you to use mindfulness to help you overcome any obstacle that comes your way.

Peace and blessings,

Dr. Cenell Boch

CHAPTER ONE
BACKGROUND

Don't die with your music still in you.

—Dr. Wayne Dyer

Health and Wellness, both physical and mental, have always been a big part of my life, and for several decades also part of my professional life. Today, in addition to being a college professor, I run two companies focused on Health and Wellness. So, when life hurled its inevitable curve balls, I was somewhat equipped to look at my life through lenses not as opaque as they could have been. I believe too, that because I come from a large jovial, even if at times dysfunctional Midwest Christian family, I acquired tools on how to navigate life's ups and downs.

I am the last of twelve children and considered the bubbly one. Figuring out things and coping were things I learned growing up. Trust me, I still had disappointments, pain, fears, and loss; however, I found that I also had the tools to buoy myself through the mire. Sometimes it took a while to see the clear sky once again but I never stopped trying.

There was a peace, serenity, and security that I found I could access even during "rough waters" and some of the most tumultuous times in my life. Yes, I could truly feel peace during the storm and find "still waters" amid the violent currents that threatened to pull me under. You see I've always believed in a greater LOVE, that there is something (Universe, God, Source, our Creator) that sustains us even when we are unable to sustain ourselves. When we fall, crumble, or simply can't see straight due to all the pressure of life, God is still with us. It's in these moments where I know my strength comes from pure LOVE, from our true Source. It was in my moments of devastation and despair that I reached out and even cried out to this Source for help, comfort, and reassurance. I hope the journal entries I share here in this book will help you to CONNECT with our true Source just like I have and still do. My hope is that this little book will encourage you to connect and stay connected not only in those times of despair but also in happy times when you just want a little more reassurance that Source is always with you.

My Health and Wellness Beginnings

My interest in health and wellness goes way back to 1989 when I began to reap the rewards of my efforts in middle and high school from running track and cross country. My body was lean and strong and I felt healthy. As an athlete, I was mildly competitive but as an introvert who at times could access extroverted qualities, the individual aspect of running track was more to my liking as it made me focus on doing my personal best. It was always gratifying to put forth the effort and then be rewarded by earning a personal record. It was also during my days as a high school athlete that I began to appreciate that putting forth a little more effort could pay off in big ways. Though I mostly enjoyed the social aspect of being on a team, our 1600-meter relay did make it to the state competition my senior year. Importantly, I truly enjoyed the personal aspects of individual-focused sports and what they brought into my life.

My involvement as a cross-country and track athlete taught me something else too. It showed me how important both individual effort and group effort are for the success of a team. If I scored first, second, or third place, that meant my points were added to the team as a whole; therefore, we all benefited. Competing well in my individual track events also allowed me to extend internal "applause" or appreciation to myself for doing the best I could in any given situation. It prepared me to do my personal best even when a part of a team.

Throughout my adolescence and young adulthood, I became a people pleaser and was a bit hard on myself. Typically, I avoided conflict as much as possible and that was not always a good thing. At that time, it was my nature to seek approval from my family, teachers, and peers; and I'd especially seek approval from those in authority over me (e.g., an employer). I had the desire to make my parents, my church family, and school friends happy... and sometimes all at the same time.

As a people pleaser, I had to learn self-compassion and self-confidence the hard way. Thank goodness, in adulthood, I have come to find that happiness is a choice I make daily, and it is independent of the thoughts of others. My meditation practice started seven or eight years ago. A paraphrase of a quote I love by Deepak Chopra states, "Prayer is us talking to God, and meditation is God answering." Or at least that is my interpretation of his quote. Meditation has had a profound impact on my life. It has helped me to respond versus react to stressors in my life. My stress response is calmer and I can pause and create space to breathe and think before responding. Meditation has also made a huge difference in my response to anxious situations that have been a part of my life. Meditation allows me to open to self-compassion, to be kind to myself, and to understand that in many situations there are infinite possibilities - not just an "either this or that" mentality. There may be another solution to the problem that we have not thought of, or that the situation is not a "problem" at all but all in how we perceive the situation. Meditation has cultivated the understanding that it might be how I am "framing" or "perceiving" the situation to be a problem but I can choose to "reframe" or change my perception of the situation. There are moments when I experience an indescribable peace; a peace that passes all understanding. Meditation has really helped me to clearly see the manifestations of God in my life.

When I began practicing meditation, during the guided meditation by Deepak Chopra, I hung my hat on the statement he made, "I am neither superior nor inferior to anyone and I am independent of the thoughts of others." This statement stuck with me and has become one of my daily affirmations.

College Health and Wellness Interest

My high school graduation was in June of 1989, and because I excelled in sports, I went on to pursue a bachelor's degree in sports medicine (now renamed athletic training) at a small liberal arts college in Alliance, Ohio.

As an undergraduate student at the University of Mount Union, I began to identify and appreciate my passion for serving others. As an athletic training student, I learned how to recognize, evaluate, diagnose, and prevent athletic-related injuries. Taking a course in nutrition science during my undergraduate studies taught me the significant role our lifestyle "decisions and behaviors" have on our health outcomes. I found myself gravitating to this field. There was something liberating about trying to understand how the human body works and how I could influence its outcome by helping it along.

Many in our society feel that health outcomes or risk for disease are genetically pre-determined. This is not entirely true. My class on human physiology was the first time I began to understand that genetics was not the ONLY factor that dictated if we would become ill. The fact is that genetic influences represents only ten to twenty percent of our risk for certain diseases/conditions. And even some of that influence can be lessened if we make different choices. During a nutrition science class in my sophomore year, I began to comprehend the impact of health and wellness, being fit both mentally and physically on health outcomes, genetically predisposed or not.

I can't emphasize more, the significant impact proper nutrition has on the various biological systems. There are several main biological systems in the body and what we eat has profound effects on the functioning of our body. Some of the systems include the cardiovascular system, digestive system, endocrine system, integumentary system, immune system, muscular system, nervous system, and the renal (urinary) system. They are all interdependent and rely on us as the gatekeepers to their healthy functioning by what we choose to put in our mouths and how the mind, body, and spirit interact.

From my studies, I started to see the impact our behaviors and decisions have on the physical, mental, and cognitive functions of the body. During this period of my life (age 18-21), I was just beginning to comprehend "the tip of the iceberg" of the mind-body interaction. My knowledge, understanding, and synthesis of physiological and intuitive mechanisms would continue to grow substantially over the next decade.

After earning my undergraduate degree, I pursued a master's degree in exercise physiology with a concentration in cardiac rehabilitation. It was during my master's work that I realized how much I enjoyed working with special populations (cancer, cardiovascular disease, elderly, and pediatric patients). After completing my master's degree in 1995, I went on to work on a doctoral degree at The Ohio State University in exercise science. As an exercise science doctoral student, it was an honor and privilege to work with a variety of different patients. Part of my exercise science graduate assistantship was to work for what was a new program at the time: The Faculty and Staff Wellness Program. This program was for the campus faculty and staff community in need of health support, and my position involved working at the Ohio State Martha Morehouse Outpatient Center leading group stretching for cardiac rehabilitation patients and cancer patients, assisting with teaching health education classes to patients with high blood pressure, diabetes, high cholesterol, and other chronic diseases.

My graduate assistantship experience at Ohio State University was a valuable learning experience. In addition to being a graduate assistant at Ohio State University, I also began working with the general population as a part-time employee for Columbus Fitness Consultants in Columbus, OH. It was an inspiring educational experience to work with Mr. Jerry Greenspan, owner, and Columbus Fitness Consultants.

Jerry was a brilliant businessman, and academic, and later became a valuable mentor, and close friend. He had earned six degrees relating to exercise science, biomechanics, physical therapy, and business. His knowledge, training, and expertise allowed the company to become a premier resource in Central Ohio for providing the best fitness and rehabilitative care for clients. This newly founded company specialized in personal training and advanced muscle treatment techniques called Muscle Activation Technique (MAT). As a new employee in 1997, Columbus Fitness allowed me to work with the general fitness population (weight loss, athletes, etc.) and special populations (those with cancer, diabetes, and heart disease).

Journal Entry

Career Knowledge

As I'm working on my first PhD, I learned in depth about anatomy and physiology, the biology and science of food, how nutrients affect the body, and the importance of using clinical research to improve the health and well-being of individuals in our community. During this period, I began to realize that there was an unfathomable amount of research and knowledge in the cosmos on any given topic. However, at the same time, the more we know as scientists the more questions arise about the topics we study. Another way to say this is the more we know, the more we realize how much we don't know.

One thing I notice about data-driven research is that it keeps records much like I do in my journal...only my journal entries capture my emotional state as I am writing it. How valuable are my journals? To me, they are key.

Questions for Chapter One

1. When did you first decide on your career choice, and what influenced your choice?

2. Did someone influence your choice in a positive or negative way?

3. What about your career makes you happy? If you are not satisfied, what would you rather be doing?

___

Affirmation

My personal and professional transformation is happening right now, and I am grateful.

CHAPTER TWO
KNOWLEDGE: PREPARING FOR MY LIFE'S WORK

We shall not cease from exploration.
And the end of all our exploring
Will be to arrive where we started
And know the place for the first time.

—T.S. Eliot

When I started working on my PhD, no one knew that the health and wellness industry would explode to become the one trillion-dollar industry it is today. I am still awed at Dr. Tim Kirby's (my former doctoral advisor at Ohio State University) megatrends prediction that the health and wellness industry would become a "booming industry" with growth beyond our wildest imagination.

As baby boomers get older, they become mindful of living healthier lives and they become more involved in their care. At that time, economists and researchers alike were beginning to publish notable research in scholarly magazines and newspaper articles about these boomers who were determined to live longer and were embodying the notion that they could live "forever."

Indeed, research today does show that baby boomers are the longest-living generation in history. With the emphasis on living longer and being healthier—baby boomers, along with Gen Xers began commercializing some of the health and wellness economic trends. Readily available public health and wellness information which led to an increase in health and wellness awareness prompted savvy entrepreneurs to begin promoting individual self-care which exploded health and wellness markets for bodywork supplements, healthy nutrition, and personal training.

These trends led to forward-thinking entrepreneurs creating businesses that supported behavioral changes such as moving away from eating foods laden with preservatives to eating more natural or organic foods. Health food stores catering to nature cures and natural foods proliferated, as did the exercise, meditation, vitamins, and minerals markets.

The Framingham Heart Study (Harvard) provided evidence that eating healthier and exercising were effective treatments to stave off cardiovascular disease and a way to prevent other diseases, which in effect prolongs life. A rapid increase in purchasing of health and wellness consumer products, such as special pH Ionized water, dietary supplements, and diagnostic screenings encouraged mental and behavioral pivots. These pivots resulted in changing beliefs about mortality and aging which further solidified the robust industry we now have around health and wellness.

As a twenty-four-year-old, I could neither fathom what this growth would mean for the healthcare system, nor could I comprehend the enormous impact on consumer economics that would emerge from consumers' changing and empowered attitudes toward their health and wellbeing. Likewise, I didn't foresee that a few years later I would leave Ohio State University without completing my doctoral degree. In those few years, I would become moderately depressed, and I would go on to experience several significant life-changing events.

In 1999, "life happened." I failed my comprehensive doctoral exams and was unable to complete the doctoral degree. Having always been a good student throughout my academic career, I was shocked and destroyed. I started to experience intense anxiety and depression. This was a devastating period in my life.

Journal Entry

Doctoral Comprehensive Exams Failure

My sadness is palpable but worse I have suddenly developed severe anxiety around driving on the freeway. To hear that I did not pass my comprehensive exams after all the work I have completed in the last four years is beyond devasting. I am in shock and detached. I feel completely lost. All the stages of grief seemed to be balled up into one feeling right now—numbness. Underneath I am scared, petrified really. What will I do now? Will I be able to get a job anywhere? Who wants failure, should I try to go to another school, how could my advisors do this to me, it is their fault, it is my fault, maybe I could have studied harder. Is it because I am black or female, or both? Again...what do I do now? All these questions, feelings of guilt, shame, betrayal, hurt, defeat, all these things are swimming around in my head like a tsunami. I can barely breathe the shame of failure feels so deep. I can hear my mind saying, "You are not enough, you couldn't complete the process, you didn't pass." Then I realize I am holding my breath…then I said to myself, "Breathe Cenell… breathe."

It feels like my total existence has been shattered into a million pieces, much like dropping a glass ball onto a cement floor. How am I going to pick up the pieces? Failure at this level cuts like a knife that leaves a gaping wound that I hope and pray will only heal over time.

Although I was devastated because I failed to pass, I continued with my life. Up until that point, I had not experienced any academic failure. My journey involved getting married and accepting a teaching position at a small liberal arts college where I taught courses in athletic training, exercise science, and public health. My academic tenure involved starting as an instructor and I was eventually promoted to an Assistant Professor. After moving up in the ranks in my career, giving birth to two charismatic boys two and a half years apart, building a beautiful dream home, starting a second PhD program, and having founded a non-profit promoting women's health and wellness, my marriage of almost thirteen years began to crumble and completely fall apart.

Journal Entry

What Happens Next?

It was so hard to believe that things were going so well in many aspects of my life but the most important relationship in my life—my marriage—was falling apart because we were emotionally distant from each other. During this period, I learned the very painful lesson that we are all responsible for our own happiness. Happiness is personal. The statement, "We are each responsible for our own happiness" bears repeating. It's important to realize that no situation or person can make us happy.

What happens in a relationship is that we can "enhance" each other's happiness, however, personal happiness comes from within. It took me a long time to fully comprehend the concept of happiness. So, I am devastatingly unhappy and overwhelmed. I am entering another troublesome period of my life.

Journal Entry

Thoughts about my parents, my divorce, and also my health.

It doesn't get easier because Mom is eighty-six years old. Losing Mom is going to be hard.... No matter how old our parents are we are never really ready to let them go. It's funny because I have been nervous about my parents dying and thinking about their deaths from a young age. I started worrying about them dying in middle school and high school. I guess that is what happens when your parents have their last child at age forty-four and forty-five. So, by the time I made it to high school and college, my parents were well into their sixties. My dad died in December 2003 almost ten years ago—that was hard, too. My dad died of a heart attack. It's all a bit blurry, I had just had my second son, Daniel (my dad's namesake), and about a month later we were attending my father's funeral. I am so glad Dad got a chance to hold Daniel. Now Mom's health has been failing over the last year, she's been to the doctor's office several times. In response to the recommended surgery for her cervical/uterus area, Mom says, "I came to earth with all my parts, and I am going to leave with all my parts." She seems to feel that at eighty-six she has led a full life with her husband

and twelve children. Bertha Lee is a beautiful, strong, God-fearing woman who taught all her children to both give and receive RESPECT and to ALWAYS PRAY. I am so grateful to God for my beautiful mother. She watched five of her children and her husband pass on to the other side—that's six funerals, not counting her siblings and parents. My mother is a shining example of a praying woman who didn't take any crap from anyone AND was as sweet as pie.

Around the same time that my mother's health condition became critical, I found out from my OB/GYN that I'd need to have a hysterectomy due to the size of benign uterus fibroids. But wait, I'm so young and my marriage is falling apart heading for divorce. Trying to be optimistic, what if I meet someone in the future and we want to have children? I guess that part of my life is over. Ugh! I love my two boys and will focus on them and preserving my health. It is still so hard to believe that part of my femininity and the possibility of continued motherhood is being taken away. I know this is the best decision for my health and well-being. I am under so much stress with my mother, the divorce, and the hysterectomy I can barely breathe.

This period is devastating. I needed to undergo a hysterectomy which is a life-changing serious medical procedure. My eighty-six-year-old mother was terminally ill. I am getting a divorce. The divorce, hysterectomy, and the death of my mother all happened within six months! The beginning of 2012 was quite a doozy! Talk about "hanging on by a wing and a prayer." My story doesn't end with this devastation and despair, and actually, this period of my life was my motivation to begin writing this book.

My coping mechanism since middle school was journaling. Journaling has always been a therapeutic exercise for me. In fact, I still have my journals from middle school. My first journal was an old-school-type journal with a picture of a lock and key on the front that says, *My First Journal*. It's the kind where you fill in the blanks. It is super cute and funny when I re-read it now, and that is where my introduction to journaling began. As the last of twelve children, it was challenging for me to get a word in sometimes during family conversations, so journaling became a very natural outlet for me.

There were so many times in my life when I felt lost and alone and it was the voice of a virtual stranger or someone I'd just met who would speak profound words of encouragement to me. It was as though they had some idea of my situation, but how could they because we barely knew each other? These are examples of my "God-winks" or angels watching over me and I'm so grateful for these feelings of safety and security. It reminds me of the biblical scriptures, "I will never leave nor forsake you" and "The Lord is my Shepherd I shall not want. He makes me to lie down in green pastures. He leadeth me beside the still waters."

Journal Entry

Anxiety

I don't know where this growing anxiety about driving on the freeway is coming from. I just know it's here and it's real. No matter what anyone has said to me, I can't find the calm to drive on freeways. I feel ungrounded, anxious, incompetent, and unsafe. I am trying to get to the core reason this has happened by getting professional help.

My guess is that the anxiety started around my not completing the doctoral exams successfully. I remember driving to Pittsburgh to my best friend's baby shower and feeling this wave of anxiety while driving on the turnpike, and what made matters worse was that I got lost after exiting the highway. I was supposed to follow my college friend who was driving in the car ahead of me. However, some cars got in between us and before I knew it, I was on my own on bridges in Pittsburgh, PA with no idea how to reach my friends. In 1999, we didn't really use cell phones and there was no GPS, so I remember stopping at a hotel and calling my friend's parents' house. I felt so embarrassed that I had gotten lost. One of her relatives came to get me and I followed them back to the house. Later that afternoon, I had to drive back to Columbus, OH by myself and was on pins and needles the whole way back. I just felt so alone and scared when I drove over the bridges. Every time I went over a bridge, I would remember singing "Jesus Loves Me, Yes I Know" at the top of my lungs in my car just to help me feel connected to Source. It was awful. It started with bridges, then I developed anxiety with any highway driving. Stress was building up (e.g., the divorce) and it made it even worse.

Questions for Chapter Two

1. What motivated you to pick up this book?

2. What change would you like to see happen in your life?

_____
_____
_____
_____
_____
_____
_____
_____
_____
_____
_____
_____
_____
_____
_____

3. How will you feel when that change has occurred?

4. Take three minutes and "act as if" the change has already occurred. DO IT NOW for a full three minutes. How does it make you feel?

_____
_____
_____
_____
_____
_____
_____
_____
_____
_____
_____

Affirmation:

All of life, both joy and sorrow is working together for my good.

CHAPTER THREE
FINDING ME

God is our refuge and strength, a very present help in trouble.

—Psalm 124:8

Journal Entry

Part of A Whole Universe

I realize my purpose in the world is not just about me.

"It's not about me" is a line from "The Purpose Driven Life" by Rick Warren. This simple saying struck a chord. Why? Because I am thirty years old and at a phase in my life where I have begun to realize that there is more to life than just my needs. I am a connected being and part of an ancestry. I mean the world does not simply revolve around me. Still, I am also

beginning to understand that, in fact, as a connected soul, the world does evolve in and through me. I must begin to take a closer look at how the cosmos work together.

This entry indeed made me look closer at who I am. I'm not a selfish person. I've always been pretty selfless. Growing up in a Christian home with twelve siblings, we believed in helping others and, of course, sharing. My friends and family might describe me as being very generous (or "too nice"). However, in my thirties, I became a "seeker." It was as if something was missing. I had worked on a PhD, gotten married, built a beautiful new home, had two energetic boys, and even had a happy Labrador retriever named Jo-Jo. On the outside everything seemed…well…good! However, inside I knew, mentally, and spiritually that I desired a closer relationship with the Source, the Divine (God). I felt there had to be something more. And boy, was I right. I have set a goal to write short stories where I explain something "more" that I have experienced. You'll have to wait for that book. My closeness to the Divine, involves a "knowing that you know that" everything is going to be all right, no matter what.

Journal Entry

Humor

Today my life presented me with a bit of humor and levity wrapped in with all the trials and tribulations.

I am so grateful to my family, friends, and church community for all the support and prayers during this very difficult time in my life. This is the year from hell. My mother has been diagnosed with a terminal illness at eighty-seven, my doctor says I need a hysterectomy and my marriage is ending and I had to move. I've now relocated from Canton to Columbus, OH. To cheer me up, my close girlfriend decided to take me out for a girl's day and lunch at Nordstrom Café. She wanted to take me shopping for something to lift my spirits, something girly and beautiful and told me about these beautiful new bras and encouraged me to get one. So, I proceeded to the lingerie department and the fitting expert took my measurements. Now I had assumed I was around the same size I'd always worn which was about a B cup. So, when the saleswoman looked in at me and announced, "Ma'am you're a 34DD,." I said to her with sheer disbelief, "No way, take the measurement again!" She re-measured and announced once more, "Ma'am it's the same—34DD." Now mind you this shopping/luncheon/ girl's day was an honest effort by my girlfriend to cheer me up. However, I left Nordstrom thinking, "Wow I'm already going through a divorce, my mom just died, and I'm not even wearing the right size BRA! Oh, boy!"

Journal Entry

Grief

Grief became a close companion, a feeling of being all alone in the world engulfed me after my mom passed and the divorce. Then three years later, in 2015, my boys decided to move to Texas with their father. I felt so alone. It was then that I found out through a friend at work about the two women's groups at her church one named Coffee Talk and the other Devotional Divas. It was a blessing to connect with other women in an open and unguarded way.

Journal Entry

Rumination

What's happening is my constant concern and worry about the future and it's put me in a bit of inertia and doubt. Should I give up on my dream of owning my own business? Should I just work hard in my new Columbus position and raise my boys? Will I marry again? And what about finishing my PhD? So many unanswered questions!

Journal Entry

Slow Down... and Believe

I feel like a whirlwind of uncertainty. I need to be still and slow down. This is when things become clear. I have read this statement in the Bible and other books and have even heard speakers talk about this three-step process of asking, believing, and receiving. So, I'm going to give it a try for myself. Ask, they say, "What is the next step I need to take, what action do I need to take? Then believe that the answer will be revealed to me. Be wide open to Receiving. I will put this into practice to find my next answer and then I will walk in that direction or at least take the next step.

Many times, the step was a small action like talking to a relative or a trusted friend about the situation and then begin taking small action steps toward my goal. Truly, it became clear. It was like I was being guided by the Divine to just take one step, one day, one moment at a time. The next step became clear… and then the next step… and then the next, and then the next. Again, it was as if a virtual guide took me by the hand and all I had to do was take the first step: slow down, ask, believe, and receive.

I had been missing my family and my urgency to see them was palpable. I really wanted to see my extended family. We had not been together in four or five years. We always had family get-togethers when my parents were living but with them gone, our time together became less and less. Our family gatherings were meaningful and supportive and, as I said earlier, I'm the last child of twelve children. So, as you can imagine, on any given day, large family gatherings were commonplace for us and they were legendary. Anyway, I really missed getting together and missed the feelings of familiarity, comfort, love, and laughter I experienced with my family. The more I talked about it with my friends/family the more I kept hearing them say, "Well, YOU have to create that environment again. It's up to you and you can create it. Just do it."

I shared my desire to have a family gathering and had an event at a local restaurant close to my apartment in Columbus. I went into action and wouldn't you know it, about twenty people showed up on a Saturday afternoon. I was feeling the love and at last, I was feeling peaceful.

Journal Entry

Yearning for Family Night

It was AWESOME! I gave out hugs, and we laughed and ate and enjoyed each other's company for about two hours. It was a beautiful feeling to be together and to fellowship. These feelings of belonging were something so familiar to me at a young age and I realized last night that I had lost that feeling as I grew older. That day was special. We talked about old times and new events that were about to happen. We even ate cake to celebrate a family member's birthday that fell on that day. After about two hours, we all went home, which was perfect timing! However, brief our get-together was, we were all happy to see each other and even planned to have another outing soon.

This story is just one example of how we can "create what we want" with Divine guidance. I wish I could say I've always felt this way; that I have always been confident about "creating" or co-creating with the Divine what I truly want or desire. The reality is there was a time in my life when I felt completely lost.

Questions Chapter Three

1. What is one situation or event you would like to create for yourself or your life? Give details regarding exactly when and where you would like this to happen. Is this solo or will someone be with you?

_____

_____

_____

_____

_____

_____

_____

_____

_____

_____

_____

_____

2. List one or two steps you might take toward that goal. List one step you could take this week and another step you could take during this month toward your goal happening.

_____

_____

_____

_____

_____

_____

_____

_____

_____

Affirmation:

Every situation has two opposing sides and I can choose to believe things will work out for me and my community.

CHAPTER FOUR

THE BIG GLASS
Finding Peace Of Mind With And Without Wine

And the peace of God which passes all understanding shall keep your hearts and minds…

—Philippians 4:7

My first marriage was on the rocks, and I wasn't sure if we were going to make it. It was about that time of turmoil and confusion that I began to think; *I need to write a book someday about all this.* Things had gone from bad to worse over two years and we had started the divorce process. It was so unbelievable that I was contemplating divorce, but I was. My older sister, Susan, was one of my "rocks" during this time. She is hilarious and is also my DIVA sister. She used to LIVE to SHOP. She would even shop for clothes for me.

Journal entry

Be Still

I don't know what's going to happen next. I am confused, tired, drained, and fearful. Coming to grips with the idea of divorce, I have no idea how long the divorce process will last. I don't know where to turn. My sister and I decided I would someday write a book chapter entitled "The Big Glass."

Sometimes the best thing to do is to be still. A Bible scripture says, "Be still and know that I am God." When we can be still and wait, sometimes things seem to just fall in place. I love that feeling of surrendering to the Universe, knowing that it will all work out, and then simply feeling the peace of things falling into place. It seems shortly after things fell into place that I began to feel myself thriving and sometimes moving forward at metabolic speed. Doors open, obstacles vanish, and honestly, it does seem things begin moving in divine order. It's kind of funny how I view my life now. In retrospect, I can clearly see how I have gone from years of trying to figure out how to just get by (surviving) to now living with the expectation of blessings and opportunities to present themselves as I am of service to myself and others: thriving.

Journal Entry

Coping

My sister Susan loves to shop, and we decided to meet up at a resale store to indulge and shop around. We ended up in the wineglass section. We found sets of really elegant wine glasses... and then there it was. She saw it first; the stem was twisted glass and it blossomed up into the biggest wine glass I'd ever seen. It was about twelve inches tall and four inches wide! We both looked at each other quizzically and then at the big wine glass. I bought it!

Susan had heard me talk about how confused I was about my whole marriage situation, and she also noted how I went from Ms. Positivity to Ms. Despair. Susan was used to the bubbly Cenell and not so used to the depressed Cenell. Seeing me in this state caused Susan some despair and she really wanted to cheer me up. As my big sister, she wanted to help me through this troubling time in my life—as any caring big sister would want to do. Susan looked at me and then looked back at the gloriously huge wineglass. She looked at me again and said, "When he starts to talk crazy just bring out this big glass and fill it UP." We both cracked up laughing. Susan said, "You should write a book and call it "The Big Glass." Again, we both fell down laughing about the big glass. I even started to imagine the book cover with a picture of my legs crossed sitting in or on top of a big wine glass. So funny. Then I started to think I WILL write a book someday. I shared the idea with my friend, a professor buddy of mine who is the director of the written and oral communication program at the University of Mount Union where we both worked, and she said, "You write the book and I will edit it." I'm going to hold her to that!

That Big Glass was filled many times during the next year after that conversation with my sister Susan. At one point I remember thinking that I really needed to find another coping mechanism other than the Big Glass. I mean, I've always enjoyed running or walking or doing some type of workout. Exercise has always been a great stress reliever for me. So instead of imbibing copious amounts of wine, I increased my walking routine. I walked and walked and walked, and jogged, and then walked some more. Sometimes it would be with a friend and many times I walked alone "to clear my head."

The Big Glass helped initially, and I had no problem enjoying a big glass of red wine. However, I quickly realized that feeling numb and falling asleep was only a temporary solution to the life-changing problems I was facing. So,

I came up with an even better solution; in addition to walking, I prayed and meditated and asked God (Source, the Universe, Our Creator, the Divine) to help me. I asked that I be guided to the next thing to do, toward the next action to take for the overall benefit of myself and my two young sons; I even prayed for their father. I know it sounds weird, but I did pray for my ex-husband, too. After all, we created two beautiful boys. We all needed guidance, strength, and the love of the Divine.

Now, when I look at the BIG GLASS (yes, I still have it), it reminds me of how blessed I am. It is a symbol of turmoil, tragedy, and BLESSINGS! I believe many people have had some sort of BIG GLASS experience in one way or another. It has now been many years since I've used that BIG GLASS and life just keeps on getting better.

Journal Entry

Embracing my spiritual self.
I look back and ask myself: How did I go from heavily using wine to deal with challenges to using prayer, mindfulness, and family/friend support as my coping mechanisms? It was mostly a mental and spiritual shift and secondly, but equally

important, it was a CHOICE. I decided to choose peace, and happiness and to look at the bright side of every situation. It was very challenging at first, however now it has become my way of life. It is not that I don't acknowledge the negative side. In fact, I do acknowledge that sometimes life simply stinks. Life can be very challenging and downright hard. However, I have also come to understand that there are always at least two sides to every situation. Have you ever seen a one-sided coin or a one-sided piece of paper? In life, if we can just take a step back to view both sides and move in the direction of what we DO WANT versus focusing on what we DON'T WANT, we will be more successful at reaching goals. I understand I always have a choice.

Journal Entry

From Uncertainty to Miracles

My top priority is to find the best home, under the best conditions for my sons and me. I had been trying to figure out our life after the divorce. I have been praying for a 3-bedroom home for me and my boys that I could comfortably afford and that was also close to their school and close to my job. It's always amazing to me how even during the craziest times,

HELP shows up. My uncertainty thank God has abated. I said a prayer (asked), believed it was possible, and guess what, that's EXACTLY what we got a three-bedroom townhome close to my job and within walking distance to the boys' schools. The boys were able to walk to school in one of the best school districts in Columbus, Ohio. In addition, the home was all three miles from my new job. After arrival in Columbus, I looked up to the sky and mouthed the words Thank you, God!

Journal Entry

Perspective

It was such a big relief to move successfully. I started a new job, loved our beautiful, affordable townhouse, my boys were settled in school, and I had childcare back up to boot. My sister-in-law Lorie was an amazing nanny for my boys. Life is beginning to look much more manageable. I'm retiring my BIG GLASS and I've decided to talk to family, my close friends, and Source about my challenges.

These talks happened as often as I needed, sometimes daily or even multiple times a day. If one friend or family member was busy, then I would call someone else and either talk with them or ask that person to say a prayer for me and my family. I relied heavily on my faith and the guiding North Star within me. I always felt like something was guiding me. I remember going out to dinner with a girlfriend once or twice a month to "talk" or just hang out. Other times my sister would invite me over and we would sit on the porch of our parent's home and reminisce about our childhood, laugh, and share a meal. My older sisters would talk about their current or past relationship stories and always encourage me by telling me, "Keep on living, it will get better." Help shows up in gradual small ways or sometimes in profound ways. I was going through the divorce process but I was grounded amid my storm!

It may be hard to imagine, but I am somewhat of an introvert and fully aware of the need to surround myself with a supportive community. For me that is church. Because I felt so supported I was able to confide in my church community, and without fail, they rallied around us and supported my boys and me. The boys probably wondered why we were going to so many Bible classes, Vacation Bible School, and other social church functions! They enjoyed all the fun activities and it helped keep mom sane. Between church, family, and friends, I survived.

Journal Entry

The Oprah Winfrey Show and Intuition

My sisters and I attended The Oprah Winfrey Show as members of the audience. It was a Dr. Oz segment and the title was "Do you know someone who needs a medical miracle?" I had actually written into the show about my sister, Carolyn, who had several health conditions and was taking care of our mother while working full-time. We were given four tickets to be in the audience of The Oprah Winfrey Show. After the show, my sister Susan, heard one of the producers say they were looking for people to be a part of an upcoming show. So, we both went and spoke to the producers, and turns out the producers thought I would be a good fit for an upcoming show transforming one's appearance. The show turned out to be an opportunity for me to discuss my platform for promoting women's health and wellness.

It was transformational because it demonstrated how the divine works in "mysterious ways." Being on the show was during a time when I was a bit confused and still working on my own personal and professional development. It was a dream come true because I always wanted to meet Oprah and be a part of her world.

It was truly a blessing. It involved an expenses-paid trip to Chicago for a couple of days. It was the first time I had experienced this level of luxury, between the hotel stay and chauffeurs. I remember looking out the hotel window at the Chicago skyline and taking it all in. It was a luxurious suite that included everything I could ever want. I felt like royalty.

My self-esteem and self-worth were low because my marriage was beginning to fall apart. I still tried to remain optimistic and believe that things would get better for me.

Being on The Oprah Winfrey Show was a pivotal experience for me and I left the show feeling that anything is possible.

Sometimes you just have to take your own counsel. I didn't know how much appearing on *The Oprah Winfrey Show* would influence my health and wellness career. It gave it a real boost and I still get recognition for that appearance to this day. It was inspiring to meet and talk with Oprah. I became a fan. During my divorce process, the *Super Soul Sunday* shows encouraged me and reminded me that I was not alone in my turmoil and that like me, other people were able to overcome obstacles one day, one hour, one minute at a time.

Journal Entry

Hopeful love

I am excited about the future. My divorce was final. In 2017, I met my soulmate. I call it divine intervention because we live an hour away from each other and met through one of my relatives. When I met Wayne, we just seemed to "click." I am so thankful for divine intervention and the persistence of my relative. She kept saying, "He seems like a really nice guy and you both seem to have stuff in common." He and I share the same work ethic and values. Importantly, we became best friends...and fell in love and adored each other. I am so grateful for a second chance at love. A chance that I was not sure I would ever get. I admit I did date during the six years after my divorce; however, nothing was working out. This is going to sound like a cliche, but it is true, I had a little talk with Source and said, I am done looking for someone, it is just me and you, God. I will work on myself and if it is meant for me to be with someone then, God, you do it!

Literally, two weeks later I met Wayne and a year later we were married. He is the love of my life. I feel so blessed that we have each other. One other thing I will say here is that I did have a piece of paper with things that I desired in a man. On that paper was, "A husband who loves, respects and cherishes me and I love, respect and cherish him." That is exactly the love that we share today. He makes me feel like a queen by not only providing for our needs but also respecting my thoughts and opinions in our household decisions. Each day we make sure to express our love for each other and when we have tiffs, we try to address them as quickly as possible to heal from disagreements. We are both grateful for another chance at love and we cherish each other and our blended family of five children.

Questions Chapter Four

1. Name one obstacle you have faced successfully. What was challenging and how did you overcome it?

   _____

   _____

   _____

   _____

   _____

   _____

   _____

   _____

   _____

   _____

   _____

   _____

   _____

2. Name the obstacle you are currently facing (relationship, finances, new job, etc.). What is the POSITIVE side of that situation(s)? List two ways you can move toward positivity. Remember, an obstacle may help you grow/evolve/stretch yourself.

_____

_____

_____

_____

_____

_____

_____

_____

_____

_____

_____

_____

_____

3. What are some positive coping strategies (friends, family, church, prayer, meditation, nature, going for a walk, etc.) that have worked for you in the past? How can you use one or two of those strategies now to move forward?

_____

_____

_____

_____

_____

_____

_____

_____

_____

Affirmation:

I am grateful for my community and the support they provide.

CHAPTER FIVE
FINANCIAL PEACE

Be still and know that I am God

—Psalms 46:10

God will supply all your needs according to his riches in glory…

—Philippians 4:19

I'm sure we've all been there. Trying to make a dollar stretch. Sometimes the struggle for financial peace is way too real. Financial peace and financial freedom are two of life's most important pieces of the happiness puzzle.

Here's my personal story and how I began to view financial peace differently and come to appreciate and understand that financial peace is much closer than we even realize. Now, I must tell you that I have had many epiphanies over the last fifteen years around financial peace. I've gone through many trials and tribulations which led me to understand that we really do create our own reality in life. That's a hard pill to swallow but it is very true. Once I embraced the notion that "I am the captain of my ship, master of my fate," along with help from the Divine, of course, I began to look at my financial health from a different perspective. I started to view financial health the same way I look at my physical and spiritual health; something I have to work at on a daily, weekly, and monthly basis. Financial, spiritual, and physical wellness require discipline and consistent practice. These practices need to be done throughout the journey of life. These habits must become part of your daily, weekly, and monthly healthy habits. If we are not taught the basic tenets of financial wellness or financial peace then we may end up in debt, confusion, and mental anguish. This is exactly where I found myself. It was an extremely painful situation to be in.

Journal Entry

Finance

I am worried about the move, starting a new business, and the uncertainties of life I might be financially strapped. I need to figure out my next steps around my finances and not have it consume me. I need to find financial peace. Where do I turn?

I have found a path to financial security. I approach my financial health and my physical health one day at a time treating myself with compassion and tough love when necessary. I used to beat myself up when I made silly irresponsible financial decisions. Now I treat myself the same way I would a close girlfriend who came to me for support or needed to hear a kind word of encouragement. I treat myself with compassion and understanding, and ask myself, *What can I learn from this situation? What is my next step to move closer to my goal of continuing to build wealth and financial peace?* I was newly remarried, started a new business, Wellness with Cenell, and continued to work on my PhD. At this time, I began to feel like I was recovering financially from things that had happened in my past. I watched very closely what and how I spent money. During this time, I had an epiphany regarding how much money I had made in my life up to that point. I did not realize I'd already made one million dollars. This shocked me and helped me to reframe/refocus even more on the way I looked at my financial situation.

Journal Entry

Where Did the Money Go?

Again, it's about 5:00 a.m. and I am lying in bed with a lot of things rolling around in my head. I thought about the fact that I have made one million dollars in my lifetime. It's my first million dollars! In reality, on average I have earned enough over the last twenty years of my career, which if combined, would equal about one million dollars. To be honest, I never really looked at it like that until about a year or so ago. I started thinking about doing public speaking and I wanted to talk about making one million as if it was a future goal. And then I realized I already have earned a million dollars. But where is it? Where did it go? And why wasn't I able to hold onto it? There was so much going on in my life and I've always wanted financial peace and here I didn't realize it was right there within my grasp.

Savings. That might've helped some. But I had so much debt and so many responsibilities. I had children, I had to work, I had household expenses, credit card debt, and student loans. And here I was a millionaire already and didn't realize it. And where am I now? Why do I wake up at 5:00 a.m. thinking about money, thinking about financial peace?

With all the mantras, the praying, all the meditating I have done, you would think I would be at complete peace right now. Well, there is a large part of me that is at peace. I must continue to remind myself of the "peaceful" part of me. I continue to have faith, meditate, pray, and believe that financial peace is my birthright. Just like earning a million dollars has already happened in my life, I know it can (and will) happen again. This time it will happen much faster and take less than twenty years. This time, however, I want to continue to be a good steward. I want to have everything paid in full every month. I continue to trust in my daily mantra, "I am a kind, healthy, generous multi-millionaire." This was a mantra I adopted several years ago as a goal I wanted to achieve not knowing I had already earned a million dollars. I now know it's not what you make but what you keep!

Journal Entry

Financial Solution

Every day is a new day and every day I look to God to give me strength to make healthy decisions. As a mother, I encourage my children to make healthy decisions each day in their lives. Some days may be more challenging however I try to model the notion of making healthy decisions daily. As a doctoral student, I am applying for research grants, scholarships, and a doctoral fellowship to maintain a flow of funding for my doctoral program. My current doctoral degree student tuition is several thousand dollars and it's due. Some days it's a challenge but I visualize the bill as being paid in full and I believe it. Thank you, God!

Miraculously, I was able to take a student loan. I felt more secure and in control of my finances. After almost thirty years of journaling, I realized finance is a recurring topic that has come up in many of the entries. It's a sticking point for me. It took me a while to understand that I created these situations and there is a way to maintain financial abundance and financial peace. Today I walk into that peace FULLY, and I hope I am being thought of as a kind, healthy, generous philanthropist. I claim prosperity and peace and desire to be a blessing to millions of people all around the world. Today, I can share stories demonstrating how fortunate I am to experience financial peace and abundance even during uncertain times. Yes, I am blessed.

Questions for Chapter Five

1. List 2-3 goals you have regarding finances. Describe each goal in detail. Rate on a scale of 1-10 how confident you are in changing each goal. For example, 1 = low confidence; 10 = high confidence

_____

_____

_____

_____

_____

_____

_____

_____

_____

_____

_____

_____

2. What is a step you could take toward achieving goal #1? For example, if you said, "Save more" as a goal, maybe setting up a $20 automatic withdrawal to go into a savings account would be your goal.

_____

_____

_____

_____

_____

_____

_____

_____

_____

_____

_____

_____

_____

3. Why is financial security important to you? For you, and your children, to help others, get an education, give to charity, etc. Be specific.

_____
_____
_____
_____
_____
_____
_____
_____
_____
_____
_____

Affirmation:

I am making wise financial choices and grateful for the abundance I have today as more prosperity reveals itself to me.

CHAPTER SIX

SURVIVING TO THRIVING TO SIMPLY BLESSED

Whether you think you can or you can't, you're right.

—Henry Ford

Wisdom is the principal thing; therefore, get wisdom: and with all thy getting, get understanding.

—Proverbs 4:7

I look back over my life and can see how I have gone from surviving to thriving to realizing that I'm just blessed. It is kind of wild because I can see blessings in every situation, even the challenging ones. It appears I've gone through periods where I was simply surviving,

I was just trying to get through the next moment, or the next day. It was like treading water but not really going anywhere. Never really getting any traction. I felt like I was running a marathon and consistently trying to catch my breath and there never was enough air to breathe freely. The day-to-day of uncertainty when living in survival mode can be some of the scariest times. No one enjoys feeling lost, alone, and not quite sure of how things will turn out.

The optimist in me somehow would find the faith to believe that things will work out, but there was still an underlying fear of what if, what if it doesn't work out quite the way that I think. I mean I believe God's got me, I believe that God was listening to my prayers but there is still this fear that surfaces at times.

Now looking back over my life, I realize those periods of just "surviving" were some of the times when I learned to trust God the most. I have been amazed at how things just seem to work out once I let go and surrender. It is kind of like me saying, "Here Source you do it, please help me take care of this situation because I can't do it by myself anymore."

Journal Entry

Fully Surrendering

Even in my belief, I have moments of doubt. I must surrender to the Divine and embrace the concept of abundance.

Surrendering is a key component to claiming your joy and happiness. It is challenging to do but I have seen time and time again how powerful it can be. To be clear, my definition of surrendering means to do all that you can and then when you don't see any other way for you to "do" something, simply let God do the rest. Surrender means trusting and believing that all things are working out for your good. Some motivational speakers I've heard phrase it as "getting out of our own way." As a former pastor of mine used to say, "Let Go and Let God." It's like saying to the Universe, I've done all that I can do; please God you do the rest.

Part of the reason I was able to surrender is because I'd learned the importance of prayer, meditation, and gratitude. Prayer was an integral part of my upbringing. Raised in a Christian household, my parents instilled in all twelve of their children the importance of prayer and having a relationship with God. My parents taught us to know, believe, and fear God AND that God is also a loving God.

Today I can see how I have transitioned from a survival mindset to a thriving mindset in my professional and personal life. I have come to realize the tremendous number of blessings I have in and around my life. I've gone from surviving to thriving to just feeling blessed. Blessings are around us all the time, it just requires taking the time each day to truly see those blessings. The fact that you can read the lines on this page is a blessing. Our friends, family, and loved ones are ALL blessings and that's just to name a few of life's blessings. Each day I try to remember to take time to look around and note how blessed I really am. The birds singing, my home, my family, my career, and the fact that you are reading this book, are all examples of the many blessings I am experiencing. How about you? Can you name three or twelve blessings right now? Naming these blessings and being grateful for them will shift your mindset. Gratitude warms our hearts and instantly brings us a sense of peace, calm, and happiness. It's hard to be depressed and grateful at the same time.

Now don't get me wrong, I still have moments in my life where things get tough. I may begin to feel like I'm moving into survival mode and the many projects or programs I am working on begin to feel overwhelming. My "Things To Do" list becomes so challenging that I can hardly keep my head above water. Now I understand and know that this part of my life is just a brief space in time—it's just a season of my life and my perception of this situation can shift. I've learned to take one moment at a time and practice self-compassion—to be kind to myself. I've learned to "stop and breathe." It's still challenging some days to deal with the difficult situation however I've learned that "thriving" involves both "doing" and "being still" which then allows the next step to be revealed naturally to me. It's like Martin Luther King, Jr. said, "You don't have to see the whole staircase, just take the next step."

Feelings of peace and happiness and blessing even in the midst of the storm, somehow make the storm bearable. The only way that we can experience peace amid a storm is by staying connected to our Source. Being connected to the Divine, knowing that God is always with us really does make a difference in how we deal with various situations in life. Today I feel blessed, yes, really blessed!

Strategies for Thriving

We all have moments of feeling like we are just surviving. Ways I cope with life's obstacles are through prayer, meditation, my daily walks, and staying focused on how blessed I am. It's hard to be sad when we focus on feelings of peace, joy, and happiness and when we truly believe everything is going to be all right. Sometimes I tell myself to give the situation mood or emotions twenty-four hours and it's amazing how my mind, body, and emotions may have shifted within that time. It's kind of weird really, how the mind can go from one extreme to the other in a matter of just twenty-four hours.

Another strategy I use that helps me thrive is a morning walk. I'm so grateful to God for my morning walks which is also my meditation time. I sit quietly for twenty to forty-five minutes in the morning to meditate, but sometimes during my morning walks I use that time as my prayer/meditation time. My walks on some days feel downright miraculous. Some days I venture out the door of my home to walk with my heart feeling very heavy with stress and concerns about the events from the previous day or things that might be occurring on any given day, and by the time I walk back through that door of my home I feel like many burdens have been lifted. It is that quiet time with nature, the universe, with God that causes a shift in my mindset. There is a spiritual hymn that says God "walks with me and he talks with me, and he tells me I am his own." During my walks, I truly feel connected to our Source. I feel blessed!

Journal Entry

Giving

Today I made strides toward being a blessing to my community and myself. It was a small step forward but even though I have limited resources, I put 10 percent in savings and tithed 10 percent to my church—and that makes me feel proud.

Cenell's Top Ten Strategies for Thriving and Living Your Best Life

1. **Pray**

   Talk to God or connect with Source. The most important prayer might be to just say "Thank you for another day."

2. **Exercise**

   Whether it's five to ten minutes or an hour, just exercise. There are literally a thousand reasons to exercise. Exercise is medicine. It has a lot of physical, mental, and emotional benefits. Start with simply moving your body for a two-minute to five-minute walk. Seek advice from a health professional as needed but most important is to just get started.

3. Meditate

There are many forms of meditation used by different religions but regardless of technique, the practice is used to train the mind to focus on the moment to achieve mental clarity, emotional calm, and a stable state of being. Some say prayer is us talking to God, while meditation is God communicating with us. Now I'm not saying God actually "talks" to me during mediation, however, I do believe that mediation allows for a "stillness" or quietness, a sense of peace. It seems that after meditating I'm more open and receptive to creative ideas and have more clarity about the next step to take.

4. Sleep

It's recommended that we get six to eight hours of restful sleep at night. How are you doing with productive sleep time? Other recommendations include limiting food and drink to at least two to three hours before bedtime and cutting out television and cell phone usage (watching YouTube, etc.) in the bedroom at bedtime. Reserve the bedroom for bedtime (sleeping) only.

5. **Eat Well**

   There is something to the old cliché you are what you eat. Drink more water, eat more veggies, and lean meats, and limit salt, sugar, and fat intake. It really will make a world of difference. Typically, we slim down when we "watch what we eat" as well as we begin to have more energy!

6. **Be Positive (Say out loud twelve (12) positive things each day)**

   There was a little game I introduced over ten years ago with my athletic training students when I was a full-time athletic training professor. Around midterms, my students would get so stressed out about exams and schoolwork and would get a little down. One day three or four of them were complaining in front of me about how tough their life was due to schoolwork, exams, etc. I'd been reading about the power of positive thought and wanted to share this notion with them, so I asked each student to come up with "twelve positive things about their life." At first, each student struggled to come up with twelve things but then it became a fun game, and they were smiling by the end of it. In effect, they had forgotten about their woes and were able to smile and laugh at the moment. So now I just randomly play this game with family members and friends, especially if I notice they are having a rough day or in a bad mood. Coming up with "twelve positive things" helps them to see how blessed they are. One time my husband Wayne saw that I was a bit irritated about a project and immediately he said, "Ok, Cenell, time to say twelve positive things!" We both laughed and I did say twelve positive things, starting with, "Wayne, I love you."

7. Create Your Vision Board

A vision board is simply a way of writing, drawing, or using pictures to describe what you want out of life. Your vision board is your unique craftsmanship. It can be as simple or elaborate as you like. Just the act of creating one helps solidify what you may want out of life. This is fun to do individually and/or as a family activity.

8. Connect with Loved Ones (friends, family, church, etc.)

Being from a large family, I have enjoyed connecting with family every few months for a least a couple of hours. Feeling connected to our community is important for our overall well-being. Isolation has been associated with depression and even a shorter lifespan. Therefore, connecting with others is important. Humans are communal creatures. The statement "no man is an island" is true. We really do need each other.

9. **Ask for Help**

    This can be challenging for some of us because we like to be self-sufficient, independent, and strong. However, it is O.K. to ask for assistance, in fact, this act of courage can lead to a phenomenal life. Could you imagine what a different world this would be if Martin Luther King, Jr., Mother Teresa, or even Abraham Lincoln did not ask and inspire those who believed in their mission to join their movement? We really do need each other and by helping each other we can accomplish so much more together.

10. **Repeat steps 1-9.**

Question for Chapter Six

1. What are you struggling with now that you like to work on?

2. Reimagine what this situation could look like positively. How can you take yourself from surviving to thriving?

_____

_____

_____

_____

_____

_____

_____

_____

_____

_____

_____

_____

_____

_____

3. What three strategies from *My Top Ten Strategies for Thriving and Living Your Best Life* will help you to succeed? (You can alternate strategies depending on the challenges you may have to face in your life.)

___

Affirmation:

There are infinite possibilities of how abundance and peace will manifest in my life.

CHAPTER SEVEN
WHEN ALL YOU EVER WANTED ISN'T ENOUGH

Appreciate life to its fullest... without judgement.

—Anonymous

When All You Ever Wanted Isn't Enough is a book by Harold Kushner. I read this book back in undergraduate college some twenty-plus years ago and it came to mind after I finished my PhD in 2023. Completing my PhD was a goal I've had for almost thirty years. There was always a part of me that felt like I just wanted to finish what I had started back in 1995. I've worked on three different doctoral degrees. The first doctoral degree experience was in exercise science and involved me finishing all the coursework and then experiencing anxiety and depression so it did not end successfully. The second doctoral experience was in public health, and after completing all the coursework, my marriage began to fail which led to a divorce so I decided to focus on transitioning my life and raising my two young boys at the time. More recently I successfully completed my PhD in health sciences, with the support of a wonderful family, my husband, my children, my doctoral degree advisor, and peers.

I received two offers within a couple of months of graduation; however, after talking it over with my husband and doing a bit of soul-searching I came to realize that those positions were not for me at that time in my life. Surprisingly enough, the position that I did find to be a fit was the least expected. My perfect fit came in the form of teaching at a small university in the northern part of Chicago some 400 miles away from where I live in Ohio. The distance of driving six hours, or flying one and a half hours would be a new challenge to surmount but it would be my choice.

The university is quite diverse, and I'm excited, though apprehensive about what teaching there year-round will be like and the impact of the commute on my family.

Journal Entry

Going the Distance

It's been twenty-eight years since I started pursuing my PhD. Well, I am done. As I'm writing this it has already been eight months since I walked across the stage at my doctoral graduation – it was quite an accomplishment. I've dreamed of completing the degree and thought, Wow it has finally happened. I'm complete. During these last eight months, facing the reality of searching for opportunities, sending out resumes and filling out applications has been very challenging. I have struggled with the internal dialogue and notion that once I finished the doctoral degree everything would magically fall into place within a few weeks.

Happily, I was offered a meaningful position at North Park University as an Assistant Professor in Health Sciences and I accepted. My transition to Chicago has been somewhat of a rite of passage. I have had to utilize savings and additional resources to meet my financial needs. I will say it has helped me become even more diligent with practicing mindfulness meditation, prayer, and seeking guidance from our true Source. Now I do believe that I must continually take action steps toward my goals, visions, dreams, and desires. So, this chapter of my book, which I have entitled, "When All You Ever Wanted Isn't Enough," is apropos of where I am now. I had erroneously felt that once I completed the PhD I would have everything that I ever wanted. I am finding it's just another road that leads to another road as we collect life experiences. The reality is that I am blessed and I do have everything I need.

However, I am human and still strive for things such as travel and having a cushy nest egg, and I keep reaching for the stars. All in all, I am grateful for how blessed I really am, and I am at peace with the fact that it's O.K. to continue to desire things and experiences that bring me joy. After all, this world is one of abundance.

I can't say that I have it perfect because I don't believe there is a perfect. What I do believe and can say, is that I'm still reckoning with the understanding that my life purpose and my joy can be unconditional. Whether I have lots of money in the bank or I have only a comfortable amount, I am still worthy of having joy and happiness in my life. Finances have been an area where I am constantly growing (making mistakes and growing), and I'm excited to say that I'm getting better and better every day. More importantly, I'm learning to be grateful for my friends, my family, and my life experiences for bringing me joy.

Questions for Chapter Seven

1. What are five things that bring you joy?

2. How do those five things relate to your purpose in life?

3. How can you use your sense of purpose to be of service to others?

_____
_____
_____
_____
_____
_____
_____
_____
_____
_____
_____
_____

Affirmation:

The loving peace of awareness is always with us, just a breath away. (Simply breathe in and breathe out.)

CHAPTER EIGHT
MINDFULNESS

*Mindfulness is simple in its concept;
its power lies in its practice.*

—Dr. Jon Kabat-Zinn,
Founder Center for Mindfulness
University of Massachusetts

Mindfulness is often described as a practice of staying fully present, engaged in the moment, and aware of our surroundings, thoughts, and emotions without judgment. In our fast-paced, 24/7 world, where distractions are plentiful and stress is our constant companion, mindfulness can serve as an anchor in your life—a way to slow down, refocus, and create balance. This chapter explores what mindfulness is, how it works, and how incorporating it into your daily life can profoundly improve your well-being.

At its core, mindfulness is about awareness. It involves deliberately paying attention to the present moment, and cultivating an attitude of openness, curiosity, and acceptance toward whatever appears in your mind and body. It's not about manipulating thoughts or emotions but becoming aware of them as they are without becoming consumed by them.

Mindfulness can be practiced formally, through meditation, or informally by integrating it into daily activities like movement, walking, doing household chores, or working. With mindfulness, the mind can learn to observe and not react, allowing for emotional regulation, mental clarity, and physical relaxation.

Myriad studies have shown the benefits of mindfulness for overall well-being. Neuroscientific research shows that practicing mindfulness can lead to changes in the brain, particularly in areas related to attention and self-awareness. It has been shown to reduce the size of the amygdala (the brain's fear center) while increasing the density of the prefrontal cortex, which is associated with empathy, decision-making, and problem-solving.

Mindfulness activates the body's parasympathetic nervous system—the "rest and digest" state—relaxing and reducing stress hormones. It has been linked to lower blood pressure, stronger immune function, and better quality of sleep.

How Mindfulness Can Improve Your Life

1. **Reduces Stress and Anxiety** One of the most well-known benefits of mindfulness is its ability to reduce stress and anxiety. By focusing on the present moment, we break the cycle of rumination, where we get caught in overthinking or worrying about the future. This creates mental space, allowing us to respond to challenges with a clearer, more balanced perspective.

   Practicing mindfulness can help us manage emotional responses, leading to greater resilience in the face of difficulties. Instead of reacting impulsively or being consumed by negative emotions, mindfulness teaches us to acknowledge our feelings and choose how we respond to them.

2. **Enhances Emotional Regulation** Emotions can be overwhelming, especially in high-pressure situations or when faced with personal challenges. Mindfulness

teaches us to observe our emotions without immediately reacting. This non-judgmental awareness allows us to understand our emotional triggers and patterns more deeply.

Over time, mindfulness helps build emotional intelligence, improving our ability to deal with relationships, communicate effectively, and cultivate empathy. As we become more attuned to our inner emotions, we can create a sense of balance, even in the midst of emotional turbulence.

3. **Improves Focus and Concentration** In an era of constant notifications and distractions, our ability to focus has diminished significantly. Mindfulness trains the brain to concentrate on one thing at a time, sharpening our attention span. This can enhance productivity and improve problem-solving abilities, as we become more adept at staying present with tasks and less prone to multitasking.

   Whether you're studying, working, or engaging in creative activities, mindfulness helps you bring your full attention to the task at hand, leading to better results and a deeper sense of satisfaction.

4. **Promotes Better Sleep** Insomnia or restless nights often stem from an overactive mind. Mindfulness

can help calm mental chatter by focusing on breath, body sensations, or simply observing thoughts without attachment. This shift in attention helps signal to the body that it's time to relax, making it easier to fall asleep and stay asleep.

Regular mindfulness practice has been shown to improve sleep quality and reduce symptoms of insomnia. By letting go of the day's stresses and worries, you can enter a state of deep rest and rejuvenation.

5. **Encourages Greater Self-Awareness** Mindfulness provides a window into our inner world. As we practice observing our thoughts, emotions, and bodily sensations, we begin to understand ourselves on a deeper level. This self-awareness can reveal unconscious habits, patterns of thinking, or behaviors that may be holding us back.

   Through this greater understanding, mindfulness offers the opportunity for personal growth. It allows us to cultivate qualities such as patience, kindness, and gratitude, which can positively impact our overall well-being and relationships with others.

6. **Encourages Mindful Living** Beyond formal meditation, mindfulness can be woven into the fabric of everyday life. Whether it's savoring the taste of

food, feeling the warmth of the sun on your skin, or listening attentively to a friend, mindful living allows us to appreciate the richness of each moment. It invites us to slow down, deepen our experiences, and connect more fully with ourselves and others.

Mindful living also helps us cultivate gratitude and a sense of presence in our interactions. By practicing mindfulness in our conversations, we become better listeners, more compassionate communicators, and more attuned to the needs of others.

How to Cultivate Mindfulness in Your Life

1. **Start Small** You don't need to dedicate hours to meditation to experience the benefits of mindfulness. Take a few deep breaths before starting a task or pause to notice your surroundings while walking.

2. **Practice Mindful Breathing** Focus on your breath as it moves in and out of your body. When your mind wanders, gently bring your attention back to your breath. This simple practice helps to ground you and is especially useful during stressful moments.

3. **Observe Without Judgment** When thoughts or emotions come up, notice them without labeling them as good or bad. Mindfulness is about accepting the present moment as it is, without trying to change or escape it.

4. **Incorporate Mindfulness into Daily Routines** Daily tasks can become opportunities for mindfulness when approached with attention and awareness.

5. **Create a Mindfulness Routine** Set aside a few minutes each day to practice regular mindfulness meditation. Over time, this will strengthen your ability to stay present and reduce stress.

Mindfulness is the practice of paying attention, intentionally and non-judgmentally, to the present moment. Starting with just a few minutes a day, it can have significant benefits over time. Be patient with yourself and remember that mindfulness is a skill that develops with time and consistency.

Mindfulness is not a quick fix, but a lifelong journey that can have a profound impact on every aspect of your life. Whether you're seeking to reduce stress, enhance relationships, or simply live a more joyful life, mindfulness offers a path toward greater balance, peace, and fulfillment.

By reading this book, you have taken the first step toward overcoming obstacles with mindfulness. You are strong, you are receptive to personal growth...and you are resilient!

Questions for Chapter Eight

1. Ways to practice mindfulness include: mindful breathing, mindful meditation, body awareness, and keeping a gratitude journal. What mindfulness practices resonate with you?

_____

_____

_____

_____

_____

_____

_____

_____

_____

_____

_____

_____

2. List three ways mindfulness meditation could be beneficial for you.

3. Practicing mindfulness can be a very powerful way to reduce stress and improve your overall attitude toward life. Sharing the benefits of mindfulness can create a sense of well-being and community. Make a list of people in your circle of friends and family you could talk to about your discovery of the benefits of mindfulness. Then, whenever you feel comfortable in your practice of mindfulness, start a discussion with them.

_____

_____

_____

_____

_____

_____

_____

_____

_____

_____

CHAPTER NINE
MINDFULNESS OF DIVERSITY AND INCLUSION

Everyone can be great because everyone can serve.

—Rev. Dr. Martin Luther King, Jr.

There's so much to say about the topic of cultural diversity. The most important is that change is inevitable. When I moved to Bremen, OH, I was happily in love and excited to be married. Even though there was little diversity in the community, I felt very welcome. I became actively involved in leadership positions. Currently, I sit on several boards and have been invited to join in the change-making process in my village and the local county. I've learned that we are all much more alike than we are different. As a conscious leader, I lead with respect, dignity, and compassion for everyone, and most of the time that is what I get in return—respect, dignity, and compassion. I still struggle some days living in a community that lacks cultural diversity. Many of the individuals who live here have lived here for most of their lives. What I have enjoyed is the open hearts and minds that have welcomed me to the community and who now see me going for my morning walks and greet me with a "Good morning" and a smile. One of the eighty-eight-year-old elders at the church I attend, looked at me one day and said, "Cenell I feel I am a better person because I have gotten to know and interact with you." And I looked at him and said I feel the same way.

Living here in this small, rural, community has opened my eyes to how we can all live together peacefully even with our differences. I have had many more peaceful gestures toward me than negative ones. It is exactly the opposite of what society might say about a Black woman living in a predominantly rural white town however, I understand from my own experience, that love abounds wherever we go, and if we can lead with respect, dignity, and compassion, ninety-nine percent of the time that is exactly what we will get back.

I've served as vice president of our local chamber of commerce as well as on the board of prominent organizations in the city close to the village of Bremen. It's been an honor and privilege to work side-by-side with individuals where change is needed and necessary for our community to continue to grow and expand.

Journal Entry

Empowering a Community

I am giving a presentation for a global nonprofit on my experience living in a small rural town as a Black woman. This is an outstanding opportunity for me both professionally and personally because I can impact leaders from around the world.

Below are the questions I received from the moderator for my talk and an excerpt of my talk:

1. Tell us about yourself and share what you feel comfortable with sharing about your life in rural America as a Black woman.
2. What advice do you have for trying to navigate diversity, equity, and inclusion (DEI) discussions

while living in rural America, especially during these polarizing times?

3. What are your top three to five suggestions for our organization regarding engaging and adapting DEI in rural America through these times in 2024?

Below is an excerpt of my talk:

Greetings, my name is Dr. Cenell Boch and what brought me to a rural area in Ohio is my husband. We have a blended family of five children, two in college and three adult children. Previously, I resided in Columbus, Ohio, and worked in the city and the metropolitan area. It was divine intervention that my husband and I met through one of my relatives. It is a second marriage for both of us and we both have been through a divorce. When I met my husband I had been single (post-divorce) for five years, and I was quite happy with myself, and where I was in my life; however, I was open to a relationship so when I met my husband things clicked for us. At first, I thought he lived too far away from the city, and then we reconciled that we would give our relationship a shot. Soon after we got married and I moved to rural Ohio.

Resilience

As with any move or relocation we had a few struggles and challenges that we faced such as understanding each other's needs and how to communicate effectively. Another big challenge for me was making new friends. However, my personality I like to say that I am an introvert with extrovert tendencies, so it wasn't that challenging for me to get out into the community. I live in a small village where there are only around 1,500 people, maybe a little less than that, and not only did I get involved with my church I got involved with local organizations.

So, I got involved with the county chamber of commerce as well as with my local village chamber of commerce as a way to network for my business and understand the dynamics of the local community. I wanted to be able to give back to the community. I think it's important that we utilize whatever skills, talents, and abilities we have while we are on this earth to give back.

My husband's and my engagement in the community are part of my introduction to living in a rural area. There's a small Amish community (with horse and buggy) in our village and many families have been here for decades, and so they've grown up here. Some of the farms have been handed down from generation to generation.

The second question is: "What advice do I have for navigating diversity, equity and inclusion discussion, especially during these polarizing times?" My advice focuses on being aware of our human connection. Focus on our common humanity. We all want to be valued, heard, respected, and quite frankly, loved.

When I walk into a room I lead with respect, integrity, authenticity, and compassion. I tend to ask the question: What can I do and how can I serve? I know one of my mentors said this a long time ago, either, "You are part of the problem, or you are part of the solution." I prefer to be part of the solution and focus on what we can do to build each other up and serve our communities.

Therefore, when I come into a situation, I look at how I can help become part of that solution. The other piece of advice I have would involve approaching conversations from mindfulness lenses. Mindfulness evolves around three tenets of mindfulness, which are intention, attention, and attitude.

And then the third question: "What are your top three to five suggestions for our organization regarding engaging and adapting DEI in rural America through these times?" Well, first, I like to acknowledge and extend gratitude to the organization for the great work already being done utilizing a Two-Generation approach, and your work in mental health. Thank you for all that you are currently doing in these complex and challenging areas.

The three suggestions that I have are relatively simple; however, they could be powerful if they are things that haven't already been considered.

1. Connect. Connect with those in the local community and connect authentically with individuals and leadership. Ask for their feedback, whether to parents, children, or individuals who are in that community.
2. Community Engagement. After connecting with those in the community, become part of the community; this will help with being able to lead with authenticity, integrity, and compassion.
3. Leadership. Lead with authenticity, integrity, and compassion (love in action).

Cenell Boch

What I'd like to leave you with are three quotes from Rev. Dr. Martin Luther King, Jr. that have been very meaningful to me:

Darkness cannot drive out darkness, only light can do that. Hate cannot drive out hate, only love can do that.

—Strength to Love, 1963

Injustice anywhere is a threat to justice everywhere. We are caught in an inescapable network of mutuality, tied in a single garment of destiny. Whatever affects one directly, affects all indirectly.

— Letter from Birmingham Jail, April 16, 1963

I have the audacity to believe that peoples everywhere can have three meals a day for their bodies, education, and culture for their minds, and dignity, equality, and freedom for their spirits.

—Nobel Peace Prize Acceptance Speech, Oslo, Norway, 1964

Questions for Chapter Nine

1. Can you define your leadership abilities? Dig deep into all of your activities, such as business and community-based initiatives, school programs, PTA, faith-based engagement, sports involvement, charitable activities, etc. In what three specific ways are you using your leadership abilities?

___
___
___
___
___
___
___
___
___
___

2. What needs have you identified in your community, and how would you like to make a difference?

_____
_____
_____
_____
_____
_____
_____
_____
_____
_____
_____
_____
_____
_____

3. Who in your community can be your collaborators or support system?

4. How would you feel once you accomplish your goal of making a difference?

_____
_____
_____
_____
_____
_____
_____
_____
_____
_____
_____
_____

Affirmation:

I am open to exploring diversity and inclusion. I will appreciate our similarities and celebrate our differences.

AFFIRMATIONS FOR YOUR DAILY MINDFULNESS PRACTICE

Below are forty mindful affirmations to assist you with your daily mindfulness practice. Repeat one affirmation a day for a minimum of five times spaced throughout the day. Repeating the affirmation helps create new pathways in your brain to support your joy and happiness.

Once you have completed the forty days of affirmations, you can start over again to improve your resilience and strengthen your ability to overcome obstacles with mindfulness. Soon these affirmations will become integrated into your life. A proven benefit of positive affirmations is helping you cope with unproductive thoughts. They also can help you see the world in a more positive light when negative things happen.

Day 1. I am happy, healthy, and successful. I am abundant.

Day 2. I face joys and sorrows with grace, compassion, and peace.

Day 3. I am a part of the Divine, the Source, our Creator.

Day 4. We all are good people. Some may not yet recognize that part of themselves.

Day 5. We are much more alike than we are different.

Day 6. Let's start with Love. I begin each conversation from a place of respect and compassion.

Day 7. I set goals one at a time and achieve them one at a time.

Day 8. No man is an island; we are communal creatures and need each other.

Day 9. I have a growth mindset, always learning.

Day 10. Each day is a blessing. I behold my success for that day.

Day 11. I define who I am and what I want in this day and lifetime.

Day 12. Financial peace is my birthright.

Day 13. I am especially kind to myself and others.

Resilience

Day 14. I am completely "present" in the here and now.

Day 15. Mindfulness is simply compassionate awareness of this moment.

Day 16. I will remind myself to Breathe In…Breathe Out…Breathe In…Breathe Out…

Day 17. I open my heart to feeling peace.

Day 18. I am beautifully crafted and wonderfully made.

Day 19. I am strong, resilient, and grounded.

Day 20. Abundance is as natural as breathing.

Day 21. Gratitude and worry cannot occupy the same thought!

Day 22. I always keep learning and growing.

Day 23. I create my day…it is all unfolding in my favor!

Day 24. I am always supported by The Source.

Day 25. It's never too late to change as long as I'm above ground.

Day 26. I have financial peace right now, today, at this moment; and I'm getting better and better every day.

Day 27. It feels so good to be a blessing to those I serve, my family, and my community through our programs and events.

Day 28. I am involved with healthy, happy, and mutually beneficial relationships in my personal and professional interactions. I serve with empathy and compassion.

Day 29. My family is happy, healthy, and successful.

Day 30. I am grateful for guidance, protection, and safety every day and night.

Day 31. I receive/allow financial abundance in my life with peace and harmony, and I am grateful.

Day 32. With The Source all things are possible. Therefore, all things are possible for me.

Day 33. I breathe in the beauty of nature.

Day 34. On days when life becomes overwhelming, I go for a walk. I know the Universe has something to tell me.

Day 35. I listen to the powerful whispers of nature.

Day 36. I serve with empathy and compassion.

Day 37. A goal is a dream in action. Day by day I am taking action toward my goals.

Day 38. Today is a great day to give and receive peacefully and joyfully.

Day 39. I am grateful for this beautiful body I have been blessed with.

Day 40. I am worthy of a healthy, peaceful, and harmonious life.

Why Affirmations are Important

Incorporating affirmations into your daily routine allows you to tap into the power of positive thinking and make significant strides toward your goals.

Here's a summary of how they help:

- **Reprogramming the Mind:** Affirmations can help to reprogram negative thought patterns and replace them with positive, empowering beliefs.

- **Boosting Self-Esteem:** By focusing on positive qualities and accomplishments, affirmations can boost self-esteem and confidence.
- **Reducing Stress:** Affirmations can help to reduce stress and anxiety by promoting a more positive outlook.
- **Improving Motivation:** Affirmations can increase motivation by reminding you of your goals and inspiring you to take action.
- **Creating a Positive Mindset:** Regular practice of affirmations can help to cultivate a more positive and optimistic mindset.

Key factors to consider when using affirmations:

- **Specificity:** The more specific and detailed your affirmations are, the more effective they will be.
- **Consistency:** It's important to repeat your affirmations regularly, ideally multiple times a day.
- **Belief:** It's essential to believe in your affirmations for them to have a significant impact.
- **Visualization:** Combining affirmations with visualization can enhance their effectiveness.

CENELL'S DREAM

Don't let someone who gave up on their dreams talk you out of going after yours.

—Zig Ziglar

Have you ever had a dream? Something you REALLY wanted to accomplish? And the only reason you wanted to accomplish it was because deep down you feel it's part of your divine purpose? I realize my dream is part of the reason why I am here on earth. It is the reason I am breathing, have the gift of being a teacher, and be in community with others!

Writing this book has been part of my dream. My dream is to be a blessing to individuals all over the world by sharing my knowledge, promoting healthy living, and empowering people to live well and use mindfulness to overcome obstacles.

Now I want to ask you:

>What's your purpose?

>What's your dream?

Come, dare to dream with me, my friend. We all have a dream to fulfill. We have a greater purpose. Let's be a blessing to each other! Let me know how I can be a blessing to you.

RESOURCES

Mindfulness

Radical Compassion by Tara Brach

The Wise Heart by Jack Kornfield

Mindful of Race: Transforming Racism from the Inside Out by Ruth King

You Belong: A Call for Connection by Sebene Selessie

Living Buddha, Living Christ by Thich Nhat Hanh

Fear/Anxiety

"For God hath not given us the spirit of fear; but of power, and love, and a sound mind." 2 Timothy 1:7 (King James Bible)

The Seven Spiritual Laws of Success by Deepak Chopra

You Can Heal Your Life by Louise Hay

Change Your Thoughts - Change Your Life by Dr. Wayne Dyer

The Four Agreements: A Practical Guide to Personal Freedom by Don Miguel Ruiz

Gratitude

The Secret Gratitude Book by Rhonda Byrne

What I Know For Sure by Oprah Winfrey

The Path Made Clear: Discovering Your Life's Direction and Purpose by Oprah Winfrey

*And Still, I Rise (*Poem: *Still, I Rise)* by Maya Angelou

Living a Committed Life: Finding Freedom and Fulfillment in a Purpose Larger Than Yourself by Lynne Twist

Financial Peace

We Can Do It Women - Debra Morrison
(www.wecandoitwomen.com)

Financial Peace by Dave Ramsey

The Soul of Money: Transforming Your Relationship with Money and Life by Lynne Twist

Think and Grow Rich by Napoleon Hill

ACKNOWLEDGMENTS

An everlasting appreciation to my beloved parents Dan and Bertha Munford, and my eleven siblings (Vontella, John Robert, Victoria, Annie, Margaret, Carolyn, Ingram, Susan, Daniel Martin, Chester (Khalil), and Bertha Marie). Deepest gratitude and sincere love to my husband, Wayne; and to our God-given blessings—our children Richy, Daniel, Lindsey, Willie, and Samantha. Thanks be to God for allowing me to be a blessing to millions all over the world.

Thank you to Marva Allen, Patrice Samara, and the Wordeee Team for your guidance, patience, and constructive feedback on this book. Patrice, you are such a force of good in our world today and I am deeply grateful for your commitment to helping others. Also, I am grateful to LaQuantis "Q" Morton for connecting us and the work you and she have done together. LaQuantis, thank you for being a soul sister as well as my niece that God has blessed me with and has supported our divine mission together on this earth for over thirty years.

Lastly, I would like to extend heartfelt gratitude to my extended family and those who wrote testimonials, my lifelong friends, colleagues, mentors, professors, and church/spiritual communities who have supported and prayed for me. Receiving this love and support from others throughout my life makes it easy for me to reciprocate and give love and support to others who are in need. It is a blessing to be used by the Divine to show love to others all over the world.

Logo Graphic Design:
Jermel Wilkerson, Sr.
JWILKSR Design

ABOUT THE AUTHOR

Cenell Boch, PhD

Dr. Boch, with over twenty-five years of experience as an expert in the field of health sciences, is the founder and president of C&C Wellness, Inc., and owner of Wellness with Cenell, LLC. She received an M.S. in Exercise Physiology from the University of Akron and a B.S. in Sports Medicine from the University of Mount Union. She completed her doctoral degree in Health Sciences at Rocky Mountain University of Health Professions. Her research includes investigating the impact of mindfulness and meditation on reducing work-related stress among healthcare practitioners. She completed the Mindfulness Meditation Teacher Certification Program (MMTCP) under Jack Kornfield and Tara Brach. As a Leadership Training and Transformational Development Coach, she has worked with C-suite and Senior Executives worldwide.

In addition to being featured in many national publications, she was a guest on *The Oprah Winfrey Show*. She has also co-produced *Losing Baby Fat*, a wellness video for women, and co-hosted the television show, *Fit & Well*.

Dr. Boch counts it a blessing to be the wife of her loving husband, Wayne, mother of two sons, Daniel and Richy, and stepmom to three adult children, Lindsey, William, and Samantha.

www.ingramcontent.com/pod-product-compliance
Ingram Content Group UK Ltd.
Pitfield, Milton Keynes, MK11 3LW, UK
UKHW021354100425
5429UKWH000045B/701